圜橋教澤

逝去的风韵
——德国摄影师镜头下的老北京

Twilight of the Imperial Capital:
Peking through the Lens of Heinz von Perckhammer

国家图书馆古籍馆　编

国家图书馆出版社

图书在版编目（CIP）数据

逝去的风韵：德国摄影师镜头下的老北京 / 国家图书馆古籍馆编. -北京：国家图书馆出版社，2011.12
ISBN 978-7-5013-4715-5

Ⅰ. ①逝… Ⅱ. ①国… Ⅲ. ①北京市－地方史－史料－图集 Ⅳ. ①K291-64

中国版本图书馆CIP数据核字(2011)第259516号

书　　名　逝去的风韵——德国摄影师镜头下的老北京
编　　者　国家图书馆古籍馆 编
责任编辑　孙　彦　王燕来
装帧设计　九雅工作室

出　　版　国家图书馆出版社（100034 北京市西城区文津街7号）
发　　行　（010）66139745,66175620,66126153
66174391（传真），66126156（门市部）
E-mail　cbs@nlc.gov.cn（投稿）
Website　www.nlcpress.com→投稿
经　　销　新华书店
印　　刷　北京信彩瑞禾印刷厂
开　　本　787×1092　12开
印　　张　11.5
版　　次　2011年12月第1版　2011年12月第1次印刷

书　　号　ISBN 978-7-5013-4715-5
定　　价　260.00元

编委会名单

目　录

Content

前　言

自从1860年英国人费利斯・比托拍摄了第二次鸦片战争场景，留下了中国系列照片影像以后，很多外国旅华摄影师都用手中的镜头记录了一段特定视野中的中国历史。从1860年第二次鸦片战争末期到20世纪30年代，西方人拍摄的风景、建筑、人物和历史事件等各种题材的老照片，向世人展示了神秘面纱下的东方神韵。

本次展览“逝去的风韵——德国摄影师镜头下的老北京”中所展示的老照片均来自德国摄影师汉茨・冯・佩克哈默。1913年，身为水兵的汉茨随奥地利战列舰“伊利莎白皇后号”远航来到中国，此后，他在这个古老的东方国度淹留十年之久，拍摄了大约15000帧有关中国的照片。

本次展出的老照片均摄于1914年至1927年。1911年，辛亥革命推翻了清朝的封建统治，中国各地激荡着革命的洪流，北京在传统与现代的裂变中举步维艰。当皇家的光环渐渐消散之时，汉茨・冯・佩克哈默透过镜头记录了古都北京的另一番景象：北京城如惯性一般依然沉浸在旧式王朝的睡梦中，上至末代皇帝和贵族阶层，下至社会最底层的普通劳动者，仍然遵循既有的生活轨道默默行走，正如同二百年来一直在玉泉山拱桥下默默往返的送水驼队一般；同时，西洋文化也润物无声地进入了这座古老而迷离的城市，悄然地植入百姓日常生活，传统与现代以自有的方式相遇并融合，就好像哈德门附近使馆区小洋楼和老北京四合院自然而和谐的毗邻。

汉茨・冯・佩克哈默出身摄影师之家，他的作品充满了鲜明的个人特色，选景、构图以及对瞬间的捕捉均独具慧眼，而其对京城各色市井人物的特写最为动人心弦：端着一只冒热气儿的大口碗的路边摊贩；围在火堆旁休憩的下层百姓；坐在路边聚精会神绱鞋的老妇人；牵着骆驼的老者……这些平凡老北京人身上所展现的不仅仅是生活的艰辛，更有积极面对困境的乐观心态。尽管汉茨・冯・佩克哈默镜头下的北京只有黑白灰，但是生动的人物和端庄的建筑却在黑白光影中愈发地鲜活起来。纵使当年有限的摄影技术无法呈现这座城市的色彩，却也难以掩盖这古城骨子里散发出的流光溢彩的美丽。这是一座沉静内敛的城市，日复一日，来自世界各地的各色人物在城中川流不息，各种异国文化也在此地激荡不止，但北京城仍然温柔而坚定地固守着自己的本色。

照相术的发明使得人们和他所见的景物之间的时空距离一下拉近了，人们终于可以几乎毫无损失地保存下他彼时彼刻眼前的景象。看上去，摄影似乎是最客观的艺术形式之一，因为镜头只能捕捉真实的存在，丝毫不能掺假。但是，无数的摄影作品证明了摄影也可以是主观的，或者说摄影是一种非常个性化的、带有主观色彩的艺术形式。照片虽然表现的是一个静止的瞬间，但是选择哪个瞬间按下快门、取景框对准哪里的风景以及以何种方式冲印出来都完全取决于摄影师的专业素养。因此，一张相片不仅讲述了它所拍摄的对象的故事，更浸透了摄影师的感性情感和艺术判断。此外，欣赏相片的人也会因其个人的原因有着不同的感受，由于立场、观点的差异，同样的景色会唤起人们心中那份只属于自己的隐秘回忆，一百个人心中有一百个哈姆雷特，这个道理同样适用于摄影作品。无论是相片产生的瞬间，抑或是观众在看到相片的瞬间，这一刻都与他们过往历史中的某种经验紧密相联，再没有另一个瞬间可以替代。我们希望本次展览的每一幅老照片都能引起观众心中那最深处关于北京关于过去的共鸣。

正是得益于所有像汉茨·冯·佩克哈默先生这样的旅华外国摄影师，以及像本次展览的合作者阿勒都·卡戴里诺先生这样的文化工作者，我们才能够穿越时空再次领略用摄影技术封存的老北京城的风韵。无论历史如何变迁，北京以其不变的胸怀包容着一切。“爱国、创新、包容、厚德”的北京精神经过历史的沉淀慢慢渗透进城市的血脉，使北京逐渐向着世界城市发展。

编　者

Preface

After the Englishman Felice Beato took a series of photographs about the Second Opium War in China in 1860, many foreign photographers recorded Chinese life and history by the camera from their own perspective. From the last year of the Second Opium War in 1860 to 1930s, western photographers had taken a lot of old photographs, which involved in various topics such as landscapes, constructions, portraits and important events, reflecting the mysterious aura of this oriental empire.

All the photographs presented in the exhibition "*Twilight of the Imperial Capital: Peking through the Lens of Heinz von Perckhammer*" were taken by German photographer Heinz von Perckhammer. In 1913 Mr. Perckhammer came to China as a sailor of Austrian warship "S.M.Elisabeth". After more than ten years, when he left this ancient country, he had taken about fifteen thousand photographs about China.

All the photographs shown here were taken between 1914 and 1927. The 1911 Revolution overturned the feudality of the Qing Government and spread fast all over China. Beijing, the capital of the collapsed Qing Dynasty, was undergoing too much during the transition from a traditional society to a modern city. When the halo of imperial capital was fading away, Beijing showed her unique scenery: the city still didn't want to wake up from her golden dream. From the last emperor and the noblemen to the humblest labourers of the low class, all the people kept moving on in their previous orbits, just like the camel caravan which had fetched and sent water crossing through the city in silence year by year; at the same time, the modern western culture had been penetrating into the traditional Chinese life. The cultural fusion took place as naturally as the foreign building of the Legislation Quarter coexisted with the Chinese yard near Ha-ta-men.

Due to his origins of a photographer family, the works of Heinz von Perckhammer possess the character of his personality with creative view and conception. The most touching part is the close-ups of the common people in daily life: a vendor drinking hot soup in the street, a group of coolies resting around the fire, an old woman sewing shoes at the corner of the city wall, a walking camel driver...they are showing not only the tough life of the Beijing people, but also their optimist attitudes. Although the photographs are monochrome, the persons and constructions in the pictures seem to come alive. Even if the city is out of colour because of the limited photographic technique then, it's hard to hide its dazzling soul. In Beijing various people from all over the world came to the city and left, bringing in their culture and faith. Anyway, Beijing had maintained her personalities while she experienced the changes.

The invention of photography makes people much closer to the things they see both in sense of time and space. Photograph seems like the most objective art, because it is thought that cameras never lie and can only take the real existence. However, lots of photographic master pieces declare the subjectivity of this kind of art. The forms could be very individual and personal. Although the picture shows a still moment, the time and scene that chosen to shoot, and the way chosen to print the films depend on the accomplishment of the photographers. Therefore, a photograph not only tells the story of its object but also includes the emotion of the one who take it. Furthermore, the one who is staring the photograph may have his own feeling according to his own history. It is said that there are a thousand Hamlets in a thousand people's eyes, so as to the photography. Due to the difference of position and conception the same scenery may call up different memories. Anyway, no matter when the photograph is produced or when it is viewed the very moment is connecting the photo with their past history. So the moment is irreplaceable. We sincerely hope each photograph existing here could touch your souls with something about old Beijing.

Thanks to Heinz von Perckhammer and all the foreign photographers, who left many great works, as well as the cross-cultural workers, in particular to Mr. Aldo Caterino, who loves China and has done a great help with the joint-exhibition, we have the opportunity of appreciating the fading charm of old Beijing through old photographs. No matter how the circumstances change, Beijing never gives up her personality but always keep moving on. The Beijing's Spirit “Patriotism, innovation, inclusion and social morals” is infiltrating into the vein of the city, leading Beijing to become a global city.

幸运的联结

阿勒都·卡戴里诺

有时候生活中的意外发现会促成一个有趣项目。在我身上就发生这样一件事：一个阳光明媚的下午，我在佛罗伦萨的古玩市场上幸运地发现了一捆珍贵的照片。它们是关于中国和北京的，约有200张，裱糊在坚硬的薄纸板上，而且几乎所有照片都是深棕色的。很明显，这些照片的年代已经久远，但却依然十分清晰。照片的卖家已与我相识多年，对于我热衷照片和中国题材的图籍这一点，他十分了解。他向我极力推荐这些照片。我们经过了反复的讨价还价，最终成交。一回到家，我就开始一张一张仔细地欣赏这些照片，从前拍摄的照片依然如此迷人。即使是粗略一瞥，也能看出来这些照片出自名家之手，并不是某个业余的游客拍摄的。适当的镜头、精心的取景、完美的拍摄：这一定是一位专业的摄影师。

从那时起，他激起了我的好奇心去探寻是谁拍摄了这些照片以及为什么拍摄这些照片。经过仔细地搜索，我终于发现了作者的踪迹，并因此而激动不已：他就是汉茨·冯·佩克哈默。汉茨·冯·佩克哈默，1895年生于米兰上阿迪杰（当地居民称南蒂罗尔），1965年卒于此地，该城原属奥匈帝国领土，在一战后成为意大利领土。我还发现这些照片是为一本关于北京的影集所拍摄，以满足挑剔的环球旅行家或高雅的游客的需求，并于1928年由阿尔贝图斯出版社在柏林出版。

机缘巧合，我在同一个卖家处买到了这本影集的参考书——一本印刷精美的影印书，在我的个人收藏中我尤以为傲。看着这些美丽的照片，我心生一念，想与中国国家图书馆合作举办一个关于19世纪20年代喧嚣中的北京图片展，这将是把这些照片展示给中国读者的最好方式。19世纪20年代，不仅之于中国，对于全世界来说，都是一段重要时期。实际上，恰恰在1928年北京失去了首都的头衔，而位于中部扬子江畔的南京暂时取而代之。因为当时国民党已无力控制北方各省，当地军阀相互争斗，并且反对当局政府。

1911年辛亥革命之后，宣布成立中华民国，先前的权力系统出现了问题，而由于国民政府无法平衡各方政治势力，中国实际上陷入了长达数年的内战和动荡。直至1924年，已退位的清朝末代皇帝溥仪仍继续住在紫禁城中，被无数奴才、妃嫔围绕着，就好像时间仍停留在从前。尽管满洲贵族已经不再统治中国，但那些满洲人仍可以继续享受某种与时代脱节的特权。北京则在1900年义和团运动失败后被欧洲势力以及日本、美国等列强侵入，千疮百孔、疮痍满目。中国的其他地方则被卷入

另一种洪流，无序的混战促使法律公平的缺失，它对君权来说是一种沉重打击，同时也冲蚀着中国这样的有着悠久文明的国家。

庚子事变55天的围困，使得位于旧城区的使馆区遭到毁坏，此后这些建筑已经重新建起，它时刻提醒着各个外国使馆，这一切都是得之于战争赔款。而北京城仍然保持着她几个世纪不变的美誉——“中国的心脏”，尽管1928年以后它已不再是首都，她不仅仍是政治权力的中心，也是经济、社会和文化权力的中心，就像北极星一般，所有一切都围绕着她旋转，好像仍停留在那伟大的天朝皇帝梦之中。

城墙和它那巨大的城门复苏，城市的大道和老城内的胡同也被光鲜、快乐的生活气息所感染活跃起来，完全沉浸在一种传统的气氛中，似乎存在某种永恒的、亘古的东西，街道上代表着不变的旧中国的各色人物鲜活起来。尽管早已时过境迁，但他们仍保持自我，似乎要把周围的一切同化。紫禁城化身为一个可以自由参观的博物馆，散发着一种带有皇室威严的光辉，就好像在那里居住了几个世纪的明清两朝的皇帝正聚在其中注视着中国的新生。

且不说那些人来人往的大街，大部分道路仍然是没有铺好的土路，数不清的寺院在一大片低矮的平房院落中间拔地而起，而那象征权力的宫殿，尽管已不如从前，却仍时刻准备着绽放出比以前更闪耀的光芒。如果有外国游客来到中国做一次旅行，就像在所有时代和所有国家那样，他们只会被带去参观这座故都最具代表性的建筑、人物和生活，只向他们展现京城文明最好的那一面。然而，敏锐的观察家们则会捕捉到那或多或少高贵的讯号，当帝国威名尚存之时，各国来使每年都会向世界上唯一的、真正的皇帝朝觐献礼。

汉茨·冯·佩克哈默就拥有这样敏锐的捕捉力，再加上他那德国人与生俱来的独特视角和无可置疑的摄影技术。尽管这些照片带有充满阳光的“南方”风格（我们也称之为“意大利风格”），并且偏爱具有代表性的题材，它们被认为是出自德国摄影师之手也并不是偶然。长镜头、纪念物的细节之处、被定格在情感撞击瞬间的人像，所有有生命的、没有生命的就像计划好一样穿过镜头。然而，一切又是无法预见的、活灵活现的，每一个镜头、每一幅画面、每一个时刻都浑然天成。

FORTUNATE COINCIDENZE

Aldo Caterino

A volte capita nella vita di effettuare delle scoperte straordinarie che poi si rivelano foriere di interessanti progetti. E' ciò che è capitato a me in un assolato pomeriggio fiorentino quando, in un mercatino d'antiquariato, ho avuto la fortuna di trovare un faldone di stampe fotografiche di notevole valore. Erano immagini della Cina e di Pechino, circa 200, stampate su cartoncino spesso e rigido, quasi tutte seppiate e molto nitide, nonostante la loro evidente vetustà. Il venditore, che mi conosce bene da alcuni anni, me le ha proposte sapendo che sono appassionato di Cina e di fotografia insieme. Abbiamo contrattato a lungo sulla cifra e alla fine sono riuscito ad accaparrarmele. Una volta tornato a casa, le ho ammirate una per una con attenzione, restando affascinato dall'atmosfera che si coglieva in quelle immagini del passato. Anche a un esame superficiale, si comprendeva che erano state riprese da un fotografo di valore e non da un dilettante della domenica. Giuste le inquadrature, azzeccati i soggetti, perfetta l'esecuzione: l'autore doveva essere un professionista e non certamente dei più scadenti.

Da quel momento è scattata in me la molla della curiosità e il desiderio di scoprire chi e perché le avesse scattate. Dopo lunghe ricerche, sono riuscito a risalire all'artista che era stato capace di darmi tante emozioni: Heinz von Perckhammer, nato a Merano, in Alto Adige (Sud Tirolo per gli abitanti della zona), nel 1895, quando la città faceva parte dell'Impero austro-ungarico, e morto nella stessa località nel 1965, dopo che quella parte dell'Austria era diventata territorio italiano in seguito alla Prima guerra mondiale. Sono anche riuscito a scoprire che queste immagini erano state riprese per un libro fotografico su Pechino, ad uso di raffinati turisti giramondo o di eleganti viaggiatori da tavolino, pubblicato dall'editore Albertus Verlag a Berlino nel 1928.

Dal medesimo venditore, in un'occasione successiva, ho acquistato anche il libro di riferimento, una copia in ottime condizioni che è entrata orgogliosamente a far parte della mia biblioteca personale. Dalla bellezza delle immagini è nata l'idea di proporre alla Biblioteca Nazionale di Cina il progetto di una mostra fotografica su Pechino nei ruggenti anni Venti del Novecento, un periodo storico fra i più importanti non soltanto per la Cina, ma per il mondo intero. Proprio nel 1928, infatti, la città perse temporaneamente il ruolo di capitale in favore di Nanchino, situata in posizione più centrale lungo il Fiume Azzurro, perché il Partito Nazionalista al potere nel sud non era riuscito ad assumere il controllo delle province settentrionali a scapito dei locali "signori della guerra", che continuavano a lottare tra di loro e contro il governo legittimo.

Dopo la caduta dell'Impero nel 1911, infatti, il paese aveva attraversato lunghi anni di disordini e di lotte civili, a causa dell'incapacità della classe dirigente nazionalista di trovare un nuovo equilibrio politico e sociale all'indomani della proclamazione della Repubblica, che aveva messo in discussione tutto il sistema

di potere precedente. Fino al 1924, tra l'altro, il deposto imperatore della dinastia Qing, Puyi, aveva continuato a risiedere nella Città Proibita, circondato da servitori e concubine come se il tempo non fosse trascorso. E i mancesi continuavano a godere di certi privilegi ormai anacronistici, sebbene non fossero più l'etnia dominante in Cina. Pechino era stata pesantemente offesa dalle potenze europee, più Stati Uniti e Giappone, dopo la fallita rivolta dei Boxer nel 1900, e il resto del paese era stato spartito in sfere di influenza che permettevano uno sfruttamento indiscriminato facilitato dalla sostanziale impunità giudiziaria, un grave abuso contro la sovranità e l'indipendenza di un paese colto e civile come la Cina.

Il vecchio Quartiere delle Legazioni, dopo le distruzioni subite durante l'assedio dei 55 giorni, era stato completamente ricostruito con criteri architettonici nuovi e le monumentali ambasciate straniere servivano da monito ai cinesi per ricordare loro che il paese era sotto tutela in attesa del pagamento delle indennità di guerra. La città, però, conservava immutato il suo fascino secolare di "ombelico della Cina", centro non soltanto del potere politico, in quel momento in esilio, ma anche della vita economica, sociale e culturale, stella polare verso cui tutto guardava e intorno a cui tutto ruotava, come ai tempi dei più grandi imperatori delle più gloriose dinastie.

Le mura di cinta si elevavano ancora possenti con le loro porte gigantesche a guardia dei passaggi principali; gli *hutong* del centro storico erano ancora animati da una vita pulsante e gioiosa, completamente immersi in un'atmosfera tradizionale che aveva un qualcosa di eterno e di ancestrale; le vie pullulavano di personaggi pittoreschi che rappresentavano la Cina millenaria e immutabile, quella che rimaneva sempre se stessa nonostante i cambiamenti e che sapeva assimilare tutto in quanto lo faceva diventare parte di sé. La stessa Città Proibita, trasformata in un museo a cielo aperto, emanava un'aura di austera maestà, come se gli imperatori delle dinastie Ming e Qing, che l'avevano abitata per secoli, fossero tutti raccolti al suo interno per sostenere la rinascita della Cina.

Per non parlare delle immense strade brulicanti di folla, la maggior parte delle quali ancora in terra battuta, dei numerosi templi che si elevavano al di sopra di una sterminata massa di case basse con cortile, e dei palazzi del potere, simboli di una grandezza perduta ma pronta a ritornare più gloriosa di prima. E se i pochi visitatori stranieri che erano in grado di compiere il viaggio fino in Cina per puro piacere, come in ogni epoca e in ogni paese, venivano portati a vedere solo gli aspetti più edificanti dei luoghi, delle persone e della vita dell'ex capitale, con l'idea di presentare il volto migliore della civiltà pechinese, nondimeno gli osservatori più acuti erano senza dubbio capaci di cogliere qualche segno più o meno evidente dell'antica nobiltà, quando il Regno di Mezzo era tale di nome e di fatto e decine di ambascerie venivano ogni anno a rendere omaggio all'unico, vero imperatore del mondo.

Heinz von Perckhammer è stato capace di cogliere tutto questo e anche di più, sfruttando - da buon tedesco - una non comune capacità di visione e una padronanza assoluta della tecnica fotografica. Non a caso è considerato a tutti gli effetti un fotografo germanico, anche se nelle sue immagini si coglie un tocco di "meridionale" (diremmo quasi "italiana") solarità ed empatia verso i soggetti rappresentati. Le riprese in campo lungo, i dettagli dei monumenti, i volti delle persone sono colti sempre nel momento di massima espressività, come se si mettessero in posa, esseri animati e inanimati, di fronte all'obbiettivo; eppure nulla appare scontato o artefatto, perché ogni scatto, ogni fotogramma, ogni momento di questo film sembra rappresentato nella sua più piena naturalezza.

凡　例

1. 图录照片均为意大利出版人阿勒都·卡戴里诺先生个人收藏，其数字版权经授权，允许用于“逝去的风韵——德国摄影师镜头下的老北京”展览和图录出版。
2. 本图录收入北京老照片100帧，为1914年至1927年德国摄影师汉茨·冯·佩克哈默先生在华期间拍摄。
3. 图录为汉英双语。照片中出现的地点、建筑、组织名称等，均以现在通行的惯称为准，经吴梦麟先生、赵珩先生、史睿先生以及中国国家图书馆古籍馆馆员讨论考订后确认。英文题名和说明文字均根据汉文译出。
4. 图录由前言、正文、附录构成。正文根据不同的拍摄主题，分为四个部分。每部分由内容简介、照片和照片说明组成。
5. 为便于读者了解建筑形成年代，附录部分列出自唐至民国时期中国历史年表。
6. 附录中文索引按照片中出现的地名首字汉语拼音音序排列。另附原始英文题名对照索引，分别列出英文题名和原始英文题名，按正文英文题名首字母顺序排列。索引条目对应数字为两位照片号，第一位为单元号，第二位为照片序号。

Notes to Readers

This catalogue *Twilight of the Imperial Capital: Peking through the Lens of Heinz von Perckhammer* is published in conjunction with the exhibition held in the National Library of China.

1. The photographs here are from private collection of Italian publisher Aldo Caterino. Mr. Caterino has granted permission for them to be used in the exhibition and catalogue.
2. This catalogue includes 100 photographs of old Beijing, taken by German photographer Heinz von Perckhammer, during his stay in Beijing from 1914 to 1927.
3. This is a bilingual catalogue in Chinese and English. The captions with names of places, buildings and organizations appearing in the photographs are given in accordance with their present names in usual. All the photographs have been identified after discussion and research by Wu Menglin, Zhao Heng, Shi Rui and colleagues of the Ancient Books Library, National Library of China. The English captions are translated from Chinese.
4. The catalogue consists of a preface, text and index. The items are divided into four parts on the basis of their subjects. Each part consists of a brief introduction, photographs and their captions.
5. In order to help readers, the index includes a chronology of Chinese history from Tang Dynasty to the period of Republic of China.
6. The index at the end of this catalogue lists the names of the places appearing in the photographs with item number. The Chinese index is arranged in Pinyin. The English index includes both the translated English titles and the original English titles of the photographs. It is arranged in alphabetical order of the former one.

第一单元
宫阙园林

Imperial Palace

北京的皇宫御苑是多么庄严美丽呀！看，那些绿或黄的琉璃屋顶，那些雕梁画柱，那些白玉石的桥栏，那些多角的各式各样的亭子，和那些金碧辉煌的牌楼，都是多么优美的艺术品啊！这些楼台殿阁，无论是在春暖花开的时候，还是在秋风明月之下，都足以使人有身入仙境之感。多少代的诗人曾写出过多少篇诗歌，赞颂这些美景啊！

——老舍《北京》

1.1 远望紫禁城

紫禁城是明清两代的皇宫，为世界现存最大、最完整的木质结构的古建筑群，于明永乐十八年（1420）建成。

Forbidden City

The Forbidden City, completed in Yongle 18 (1420), had been the imperial palace from the mid-Ming Dynasty to the end of the Qing Dynasty. It is the biggest and most complete aggregation of ancient wooden buildings in existence. It now houses the Palace Museum.

1.2 紫禁城

Forbidden City

1.3 远眺琼华岛

摄影师从五龙亭的龙泽亭和澄祥亭之间取景拍摄琼华岛。琼华岛上的白塔为全园标志，建于清初顺治八年（1651），系清世祖顺治依西藏喇嘛恼木汗请求而兴建的一座藏式喇嘛塔。

Qionghua Island, Beihai

This picture was taken from Five Dragon Pavilions. The symbol of Beihai is the White Pagoda in the Qionghua Island. It was a Lama Pagoda which was built according to Lama Nomuhan's request in 1651.

1.4 北海善因殿

北海永安寺内的善因殿是北海最小的殿，建于乾隆十六年（1751），内供有铜质鎏金“大威德金刚”（俗称“千手千眼佛”）佛像。四壁外侧镶有琉璃小佛像455尊，华美而庄重。

Shanyin Hall, Beihai

Shanyin Hall in Yong’an Temple, built in Qianlong 16 (1751), is the smallest hall in Beihai. On its four outer sides there are 455 fine mounted Buddhist figures.

1.5 北海琼华岛

因岛上建有白塔，又名“白塔山”，岛上主要建筑有永安寺、白塔、悦心殿、阅古楼等，依山势分布，高低错落有致。

Qionghua Island, Beihai

Because of the White Pagoda, the Qionghua Island is also called White Pagoda Hill. The main buildings in the island are Yong'an Temple, the White Pagoda, Yuexin Hall, Yuegu Pavilion and some other constructions.

1.6 北海琼华岛环廊远眺

环廊呈半圆形，环抱于琼岛北麓的北海湖畔，长300米，分上下两层。照片中，从长廊可以望到北海湖北岸西侧的五龙亭、小西天极乐世界和西天梵境的大慈真如宝殿。

View from corridor of Qionghua Island, Beihai

The double-deck ring corridor lies on the bank of the Beihai Lake, has a length of 300m. From here we can see the Five Dragon Pavilions, Dacizhenru Hall and other buildings on the opposite bank.

1.7 北海九龙壁

建于乾隆二十一年（1756），原为大圆镜智宝殿前的影壁，为了镇慑火灾和辟除邪祟。两面各饰有九条形态各异的彩色大蟠龙，整个壁上大大小小则共有635条龙。

Nine Dragon Wall, Beihai

Built in Qianlong 21 (1756), it was originally the screen wall in front of Dayuanjingzhi Hall. There are 9 big dragons on each side and in total 635 dragons on the whole wall.

1.8 九龙壁

九龙壁上的九龙以高浮雕手法制成，黄色正龙居中，左右两侧各有蓝白两龙，白为升龙，蓝为降龙，外侧双龙则为一黄一紫。照片所示为白龙。

Nine Dragon Wall

The Nine Dragon Wall has the dragons made by high relief. A yellow dragon is in the center, while on each side there are a upping white dragon and a down blue dragon. The picture shows the white dragon. Another pair of yellow dragon and purple dragon is at the outer side of the blue dragons and white dragons.

1.9 北海大桥金鳌玉蝀牌楼

北海大桥东西两端各有一座牌楼，西曰金鳌，东曰玉蝀。

Arch on Beihai Bridge

On both sides of Beihai Bridge, there was an arch, called “Jin Ao” and “Yu Dong”.

1.10 地安门大街

照片中的街道是地安门大街，远处左侧为景山，右侧为北海。

Di'anmen Street

In middle of the photograph it is Di'anmen Street. On the distant scene, Jingshan Hill is on the left, and Beihai Park on the right.

1.11　国子监圜桥教泽牌坊

国子监是我国古代国家管理教育的最高机构，又是国家的最高学府。圜桥教泽牌坊建于乾隆四十八年(1783)，坊壁雕飞舞盘龙，正面匾额为“圜桥教泽”，背面为“学海节观”。

Huanqiao Jiaoze Arch, Guozijian

Guozijian (School of the Sons of State) was the Administration of Education and Imperial College in Ancient China. The arch was built in Qianlong 48 (1783) with fine sculptures.

1.12 圆明园

圆明园，原为皇家园林，有“万园之园”之称，于1860年和1900年分别遭受英法联军和八国联军焚毁。

Yuan Ming Yuan

Yuan Ming Yuan, the Old Summer Palace, has the reputation of “Garden of Gardens”. It was burnt down in 1860 by the Anglo-French Allied Forces and was destroyed again in 1900 by the Eight-Power Allied Forces.

1.13 颐和园

颐和园位于北京市西北郊，原名清漪园，始建于清乾隆十四年（1749），是中国目前最大、保存最完好的皇家园林。

Summer Palace

The Summer Palace has its original name Qingyi Yuan, which had started to be built in Qianlong 14 (1749). Now it has the largest and most complete preservation of the imperial garden in China.

1.14 颐和园长廊

长廊东起邀月门，西至石丈亭，中间穿过排云门，两侧对称点缀着留佳、寄澜、秋水、清遥四座重檐八角攒尖亭，象征春夏秋冬四季。全长728米，共273间。

Long Corridor, Summer Palace

The Long Corridor is 728 meters long and divided into 273 rooms. It starts from the Yaoyue Gate, passing through Paiyun Gate and westwards to Shizhang Pavilion. There are two pavilions on each side along the corridor which symbolizes the four seasons.

1.15 颐和园仁寿殿前的铜龙

仁寿殿是慈禧和光绪住园期间临朝理政、接受恭贺和接见外国使节的地方，是颐和园听政区的主要建筑。

Bronze statue of dragon, Summer Palace

This is the bronze statue of dragon in front of Renshou Hall, where Empress Dowager Cixi (1835-1908) and Emperor Guangxu (1871-1908) handled court affairs, accepted laudations and received foreign diplomats during their stay in the Summer Palace.

1.16 颐和园谐趣园

谐趣园位于颐和园的东北角，小巧玲珑，在颐和园中自成一局，故有“园中之园”之称。

Xiequ Garden, Summer Palace

Xiequ Garden locates in the northeast corner of Summer Palace which is small and delicate. It was known as “Garden in Garden” .

1.17 颐和园谐趣园

谐趣园中共有桥五座，其中知鱼桥最为著名。该桥接近水面，便于观鱼，故取名知鱼桥。

Xiequ Garden, Summer Palace

There are five bridges in Xiequ Garden and the best famous one is Zhiyu Bridge.

1.18 颐和园佛香阁

佛香阁是颐和园的主体建筑，建在万寿山前21米的方形台基上，南对昆明湖，背靠智慧海。乾隆十五年（1750）为庆祝皇太后六十寿辰于园静寺旧址建大报恩延寿寺，是今佛香阁的前身。

Foxiang Pavilion, Summer Palace

Foxiang Pavilion (Pavilion of Buddhist Incense) on Wanshou Hill (Longevity Hill) , built in 1750, is the main element of the Summer Palace.

1.19 颐和园十七孔桥

十七孔桥是连接东岸与南湖岛的长桥，桥栏上雕有544只神态各异的狮子。

Seventeen-Arch Bridge, Summer Palace

The marble Seventeen-Arch Bridge, which spans the Eastern Causeway to South Lake Island, has balusters topped by 544 carved lions in different poses.

1.20　玉泉山圣缘寺多宝琉璃塔

建于清乾隆年间。在造型、高度和颜色上与颐和园多宝琉璃塔基本一致，建成时间也比较相近，极有可能使用了同一图样。

Porcelain pagoda, Shengyuan Temple

The porcelain pagoda in Shengyuan Temple was built in the Qianlong Reign (1736–1796) of the Qing Dynasty. Its style, height and colour are the same as the porcelain pagoda in the Summer Palace.

1.21 香山昭庙琉璃塔

昭庙，全名宗镜大昭之庙，建于乾隆四十五年（1780），是为迎接西藏班禅六世进京而特地建造的夏季行宫，仿照西藏日喀则扎什伦布寺建造。琉璃塔是园内唯一一座宝塔。

Porcelain pagoda, Zhao Temple

The Zhao Temple is the summer palace built for Panchen Lama VI when he arrived in Beijing in Qianlong 45 (1780). Its architecture style followed the Tashilhunpo Monastery in Xigaze. The porcelain pagoda is the only pagoda in Zhao Temple.

1.22　香山昭庙前琉璃牌坊

北京境内最大最漂亮的琉璃牌坊。牌坊上部正中、两面有题额，均为汉藏满蒙古四种文字，东额为“法源演庆”，西额曰“慧照腾辉”，立于乾隆四十五年（1780）。

Porcelain arch, Zhao Temple

This is the biggest and most beautiful porcelain arch in Beijing. On the both sides of the upper part of the arch, there was separately a plague written in Han-Chinese, Tibetan, Manchu and Mongolian. It was built in Qianlong 45 (1780),

1.23 长城

长城作为抵御塞北游牧部落侵袭而修筑的大规模军事工程，始建于春秋战国时期，历时达两千多年，1987年被列入《世界遗产目录》。

Great Wall

The Great Wall is a series of stone and earthen fortifications in northern China, built originally to protect the northern borders of the Chinese Empire from intrusions. Several sections had been built since the 5th century B.C.. In 1987, the Great Wall was ranked in the *List of UNESCO World Heritage*.

1.24 长城

现存长城遗迹主要为始建于14世纪的明长城，东起山海关，西至嘉峪关，从东向西行经10个省区市，全长8851.8公里，平均高6—7米、宽4—5米。

Great Wall

The nowadays existent Great Wall mostly dates from the 14th century of Ming Dynasty, stretching from Shanhai Pass in the east, to Jiayu Pass in the west, along cities of 10 provinces. All the walls measure 8,851.8km with an average height of 6-7m and an average width of 4-5m.

第二单元
街衢市景

City View

北平在人为之中显出自然，几乎是什么地方既不挤得慌，又不太僻静：最小的胡同里的房子也有院子与树；最空旷的地方也离买卖街与住宅区不远。这种分配法可以算——在我的经验中——天下第一了。北平的好处不在处处设备得完全，而在它处处有空儿，可以使人自由的喘气；不在有好些美丽的建筑，而在建筑的四围都有空闲的地方，使它们成为美景。每一个城楼，每一个牌楼，都可以从老远就看见。况且在街上还可以看见北山与西山呢！

——老舍《想北平》

2.1 前门箭楼

前门是正阳门的俗称，包括箭楼和城楼。作为内城正南门，是九座城门中最为高大的一座，也是交通最为繁忙的城门之一。

Archery tower of Qianmen Gate

Qianmen Gate is the popular name of Zhengyang Gate. In the past Qianmen Gate was the biggest and busiest gate as the due south gate of inner city, which included a gate tower and an archery tower.

2.2 前门大街

照片为从箭楼看前门大街。前门大街，总长845米，宽21米，明、清至民国时皆称正阳门大街，百姓俗称前门大街。

Qianmen Street

Qianmen Street, formally called Zhengyangmen Street, has been a famous business street since Ming Dynasty. It is 845 meters in length and 21 meters in width.

2.3 京奉铁路正阳门东车站

自清末至20世纪中期北京最大的火车站。由英国人修建，现为中国铁道博物馆正阳门馆。照片所示为车站及站前的货场。

Zhengyangmen East Station of the Beijing-to-Fengtian Railway

Designed by English engineer, the Zhengyangmen East Station of the Beijing-to-Fengtian Railway was completed in 1906. It was the largest railway station in Beijing from the late Qing Dynasty to the mid-twentieth century. Now here is one part of China Railway Museum.

2.4 远望中华门

中华门，曾名为大明门、大清门，是北京明清皇城的正南门，在北京中轴线上，现已拆除。原址在正阳门北侧，现人民英雄纪念碑以南、毛主席纪念堂一带。

View of Zhonghua Gate

Zhonghua Gate located on the axis of Beijing. It was to the north of Zhengyang Gate as the south gate of the Forbidden City. It has been removed now.

2.5 东单牌楼

东单牌楼原名“就日”，1916年袁世凯将东单改为“景星”，1923年东单牌楼因妨碍交通而被拆除。

Dongdan Arch

The old name of Dongdan Arch was "Jiuri Arch". In 1916, Yuan Shikai (1859–1916) renamed it as "Jingxing". In 1923, this decorated archway was pulled down as it blocked the traffic.

2.6 崇文门

俗称哈德门。始建于元至元五年（1268），明永乐十七年（1419）重修。初名文明门，沿用元大都城文明门之名，后取《左传》"崇文德也"之典改名崇文门。

Chongwen Gate

Chongwen Gate was built in Zhiyuan 5 (1268) of Yuan Dynasty and repaired in Yongle 17 (1419) of Ming Dynasty. It was first named Wenming Gate in the Yuan Dynasty and renamed Chongwen Gate in the Ming Dynasty. But the local people usually call it Ha-ta-men.

2.7 崇文门外

Out of Chongwen Gate

2.8 崇文门

Chongwen Gate

2.9 鸟瞰外城

北京城划分为内城和外城，西方图书通常将它们分别称为“鞑靼城”（Tartar Town）和“中国城”（Chinese Town）。

View of the Chinese Town

Beijing was divided into two parts, the inner city and the outer city. In western literature the former was called Tartar Town while the latter, Chinese Town.

2.10 西便门及瓮城

西便门位于北京城墙西南端角楼旁边，主要由城楼、箭楼、瓮城组成。今残存城墙一段。

Xibian Gate

Xibian Gate was the southwest gate of outer city, composed of gate tower, archery tower and barbican. There is still a piece of city wall existed.

2.11 城墙

该段为北京内城南城墙，远处为崇文门、正阳门火车站以及正阳门。

City Wall

The photograph shows the south part of the city wall in Beijing. In the perspective there are Chongwen Gate, Zhengyangmen Railway Station and Zhengyang Gate.

2.12 东便门瓮城

东便门是北京外城东南端的一座小城门，位于北京城墙东南端角楼旁边，是外城的城门之一。1952年因修路拆除瓮城及箭楼城台。

Barbican of Dongbian Gate

Dongbian Gate is the southeast gate of the outer city. In 1952 its barbican and archery tower were removed because of the construction of railways.

2.13　观象台

世界上最古老的天文台之一，从明正统年间到1929年连续从事天文观测达500年。照片所示为象限仪（地平纬仪），制于康熙八年至十二年(1669—1673)，由比利时传教士南怀仁监制。

Observatory

As one of the oldest observatories in the world, the Observatory of Beijing had carried out astronomical observation since the early Ming Dynasty (ca. 1436–1449) till 1929 for 500 years. In the picture, it is the quadrant apparatus, which was produced under the direction of Belgian missionary Ferdinand Verbiest (1623–1688) during 1669 to 1673.

2.14 东便门角楼外大通桥畔

东便门及大通桥附近的水系，是元明清三代城市水网的枢纽。护城河水通过大通闸流入通惠河，故大通桥实际是通惠河的起始点，亦曾是京城水路交通要道。

Southeast corner of the city wall

Near the southeast corner of the city wall there was an area of canals and rivers. This area had been the key point in the water system of Beijing since Yuan Dynasty. It also communicated the Grand Canal between Beijing and Hangzhou.

2.15 漕运河道

漕运河道曾是旧京南北行人与货物出入的交通要道，许多江南购来的宫廷御用品均从通惠河而来，于大通桥转运至京城。

Canal

The canal formed one part of the Caoyun System in Beijing, a water and land based grain transportation system. The eastern canal in the city communicated Beijing and the south part of china, which was the imperial granary.

2.16　拉骆驼的人

自清代始北京就常有驼队穿行，隆冬时节，城内各处所购的煤，多雇驼户代为运输。

Camel driver

Since the Qing Dynasty there had been many camel caravans passing through Beijing. Especially in winter the camel caravans carried coals from the west places to Beijing through the Fucheng Gate.

2.17 拉骆驼的人

照片中是旧京驼户，孩子年纪尚小，精神焕发。驼户大都是京西门头沟一带的村民，个个体格健壮而善走，性情朴厚而粗豪。

Camel driver

The camel driver was still young and he gave a big smile in front of the camera. The majority of camel drivers was from the western countryside of Beijing. They had a strong constitution and honest character.

2.18 饮骆驼

旧京驼户须长途跋涉口外选购骆驼，并历尽千辛万苦一步步拉回北京。而且所购骆驼皆被驯服，听人摆布。因此，驼户对自己的骆驼备加爱护。

Watering place

The camel drivers had to buy camels outside the Great Wall. All the camels were well trained and easy to drive. Therefore, the drivers took good care of their own camels.

2.19 玉峰塔和驼队

玉峰塔，建于清乾隆年间，位于玉泉山主峰香积寺内，是一座八角形的楼阁式砖塔，系仿照江苏镇江金山寺的慈寿塔而建。明清两代宫廷用水皆从玉泉山来。

Yufeng Pagoda with a caravan

Yufeng Pagoda, built during the Qianlong Reign of the Qing Dynasty, lies in Xiangji Temple in the Yuquan Mount and is an octagonal brick pagoda in pavilion form. In Ming and Qing dynasties, the imperial court got drinking water from the Yuquan Mount.

2.20 经过玉泉山棂星门的驼队

驼队途径玉泉山麓附近的汉白玉双石牌坊，往颐和园方向前进。两座牌坊中间是一座桥，是由玉泉山取水送往皇宫的必经之路。

Camel caravan near the Yuguan Mount

The camel caravan was passing through the double stone arches near the Yuquan Mount, in the direction of the Summer Palace. There was a bridge between the two arches, along which it was the only way to get water from the Yuquan Mount for the imperial court.

2.21 玉泉山附近的石拱桥

Stone arch bridge near Yuquan Mount

2.22 青龙桥火车站台

1905年，京张铁路局总工程师詹天佑带领1万多人，仅用4年时间建成长达200余公里的京张铁路。这是首条由中国人自行设计、建造的铁路。

Qinglong Bridge Railway Station

The chief engineer of Beijing-to-Zhangjiakou Railway was Zhan Tianyou (1861-1919), a Yale graduate majoring in civil and railway engineering. This railway was famous as the first railway which was designed and built by Chinese engineer.

第三单元
寺庙宫观

Religious Architecture

城内城外有许多寺院开放，任人游览，小贩们在庙外摆摊，卖茶、食品和各种玩具。北城外的大钟寺，西城外的白云观，南城的火神庙（厂甸）是最有名的。可是，开庙最初的两三天，并不十分热闹，因为人们还正忙着彼此贺年，无暇及此。到了初五六，庙会开始风光起来，小孩们特别热心去逛，为的是到城外看看野景，可以骑毛驴，还能买到那些新年特有的玩具。白云观外的广场上有赛轿车赛马的；在老年间，据说还有赛骆驼的。这些比赛并不争取谁第一谁第二，而是在观众面前表演骡马与骑者的美好姿态与技能。

——老舍《北京的春节》

3.1 天坛祈年殿

天坛，始建于明朝永乐十八年（1420），是中国明清两朝历代皇帝祭天之地。祈年殿是天坛的主体建筑，又称祈谷殿，是明清两代皇帝孟春祈谷之所。

Qinian Hall, Temple of Heaven

The Temple of Heaven was constructed in Yongle 18 (1420) of Ming Dynasty. The Qinian Hall (Hall of Prayer for Good Harvests) is the main building of the Heaven Temple where the emperor prayed for good harvests.

3.2 天坛棂星门

棂星门位于皇穹宇北侧。皇穹宇是放置皇天上帝和皇帝祖先牌位的地方。

Lingxing Gate, Temple of Heaven

Lingxing Gate is in the north of Huangqiongyu (Imperial Vault of Heaven), which is the place to lay the memorial tablets of god and imperial ancestores.

3.3 影壁砖雕

影壁，也称照壁，是中国传统建筑中用于遮挡视线的墙壁。影壁通常装饰有很多吉祥图案的砖雕。

Screen wall

The screen wall, also called spirit wall, was used to shield an entrance gate in traditional Chinese architecture. Usually the screen wall was well decorated with brick sculpture.

3.4 清碑

驮石碑的巨兽叫做赑屃，相传为龙之九子之一，又名霸下。形似龟，擅负重，长年累月地驮载着石碑，在庙院祠堂里随处可见。

Tortoise monument

The animal used as a pedestal of the tortoise monument is called Bixi or Baxia, one of the nine "children of the dragon". It looks like tortoise and adapt to carrying heavy load. Bixi can be easily found in temples and ancestral halls.

3.5 戒台寺

本名为“万寿寺”，始建于唐代武德年间（618—626），位于京郊门头沟区永定镇南部马鞍山麓，以拥有中国最大的戒台而闻名。

Jietai Temple

Jietai Temple, originally named Wanshou Temple, is a Buddhist temple in Mentougou District in western Beijing. It was constructed during the Wude Reign (618-626) of Tang Dynasty, with major modifications made during the Ming and Qing dynasties.

3.6 戒台寺方丈

方丈就是一寺之住持，即寺中的最高领导者。《维摩诘经》记载维摩诘居士所住的卧室虽仅一丈见方却容纳广大，佛教用“方丈”命名住持的居室，后也以此称呼住持本人。

Fang Zhang of Jietai Temple

The word “Fang Zhang” means Buddhist abbot. Fang Zhang firstly referred to the living room of Buddhist abbot, meaning containing more than the real room space. Gradually, “Fang Zhang” is used as the title of Buddhist abbot.

3.7 和尚

Monk

3.8 读经僧人

A learned monk

3.9 真觉寺金刚宝座塔

真觉寺，俗称五塔寺，位于西直门外白石桥以东长河北岸，创建于明代永乐年间(1403—1424)。金刚宝座塔是中国佛塔的主要形式之一，特点是在高大的台基上建有五座佛塔。

Five-Towered Pagoda, Zhenjue Temple

The Five Tower Temple, formally known as the Zhenjue Temple (Temple of the Great Righteous Awakening), is a Buddhist temple built during Yongle Reign (1403–1424) of Ming Dynasty.The Five-Towered Pagoda has a square foundation, which supports five towers and a glazed pavilion.

3.10 碧云寺

位于京城西郊香山北隅，始建于元代，是北京著名古刹，风景优美，素有“园中之园”之称。

Biyun Temple

The Biyun Temple (Cloister of the Emerald Clouds) is a Buddhist temple located in the western part of the Xiangshan Hills, just outside the north gate of Xiangshan Park (Fragrant Hills Park). It was built in the Yuan Dynasty.

3.11 碧云寺山门

山门，又称“三门”，是汉传佛教寺院的正门，三个门洞象征着智慧、慈悲、方便三解脱门之义，或象征信、解、行三者。

Gate of Biyun Temple

This is the gate of the temple. In Chinese Buddhism, the three arches of the gate symbolize three Buddhist notions.

3.12　弥勒佛

弥勒佛，与燃灯佛、释迦牟尼佛并称三世佛。中国人认为五代时期的布袋和尚是弥勒佛转世，于是就有了喜笑颜开的大肚弥勒佛形象，在汉传佛教中影响很大。

Mile Fo

Mile Fo is the Chinese name given to Maitreya. The Chinese monk Budai has been popularly regarded as an incarnation of the bodhisattva Maitreya. His depiction as the laughing Buddha continues to be very popular in Chinese Buddhist culture.

3.13 黑寺法事活动

黑寺曾是北京著名的喇嘛庙，位于现今海淀区马甸一带，以春节期间的打鬼祭祀活动闻名，1925年毁于军阀混战，故而这张照片更显珍贵。

Procession in the Black Temple

The Black Temple was one of the famous Lama Temples in Haidian District of Beijing, which used to have activities of beating ghosts during Spring Festival. It was destroyed in 1925 during the Civil War. So now nothing exists.

3.14 黄寺清净化城塔

黄寺是北京著名的藏传佛教寺院。建于清顺治八年(1651)，是清王朝为西藏宗教领袖达赖五世修建的。

Qingjing Huacheng Pagoda, Yellow Temple

The Yellow Temple is a famous Tibetan Buddhist temple in Beijing which founded by the Qing Emperor Shunzhi in 1651 for Tibetan religious leader.

3.15 黄寺塔座石雕
Stone engraving of pagoda basement, Yellow Temple

3.16　黄寺四大天王

Four Heavenly Kings in Buddhism, Yellow Temple

3.17 十方普觉寺卧佛

十方普觉寺俗称卧佛寺，位于北京西郊香山，是京城著名佛寺。始建于唐代。寺中有元代铸造的卧佛像。

The Sleeping Buddha

The Sleeping Buddha Temple has its original name of Shifang Pujue Temple, which was built in the Tang Dynasty (7th Century). It is best known as the location of the Recumbent Buddha, a large sculpture of the Sleeping Buddha created in Yuan Dynasty.

3.18 石雕前的僧人

Monk before stone sculpture

3.19　寺庙看守

佛教寺院中的僧侣有严格的分工，每个僧人都有自己的职守，这张照片上是被称为“夜巡”的僧人，专门负责夜警巡视、每天清晨敲木板催醒众僧。

The temple guardian

There is a strict division of different levels of Buddhist monks in monastery. The monk in the photograph is in charge of "Night Watch". Every morning he wakes others up by knocking on a piece of wood.

3.20 道士

道士是对道教出家修行者的通称，别称“黄冠”、“羽客”，作为中国土生土长的唯一宗教，其装扮采用了汉族传统服饰，但头上所戴的道巾表明了其宗教身份。

Taoist mendicant friar

Taoist refers to a priest in Taoism, which is generally called Daoshi. Taoist is also called as “Huang Guan”(yellow hat) and “Yu Ke”(feather man) in Chinese. Their cloth has a traditional Han style with a scarf in head.

3.21 穿百衲衣的道士

道士为了表示苦修，拾取别人丢弃的陈旧杂碎的布片，洗涤干净后，加以密缝拼缀而成的衣服，即为百衲衣。

Taoist wearing Baina Robe

The special dress of Taoist, the Baina robe, comes from the idea of self-torture. They often make Baina robes from pieces of abandoned cloth by cleaning and sewing them together.

3.22 僧人叩拜
Monk sacrificing

3.23 万寿寺藏经楼及叠石

万寿寺建于明万历五年（1577），由万历皇帝之母慈圣李太后出资建成，清代曾两次扩建，成为清代皇家祝寿庆典的重要场所。

Classic Hall, Wanshou Temple

Wanshou Temple (Temple of the Ten Thousand Ages) was first built in 1577 by Empress Dowager Cisheng (mother of Ming Emperor Wanli). In Qing Dynasty it had been expanded twice and became the important place for offering birthday celebrations for imperial family.

3.24 寺庙一角
Corner view in a temple

3.25 寺院雪景

Snow scene in a temple

3.26　寺庙中的跨院

Buildings in a temple

3.27 礼拜寺

此礼拜寺充分吸收汉族建筑艺术特色，形成别具一格的中国式礼拜寺建筑。

Mosque

The mosques in Beijing did not replicate many of the features which often associated with traditional mosques. Instead, they followed traditional Chinese architecture.

3.28 雍和宫

雍和宫本是清雍正皇帝登基之前的府邸，后改建为喇嘛庙，成为北京城最负盛名的藏传佛教寺庙。寺中的檀木大佛高26米，是中国现存最大的木雕佛之一。

Yonghe Temple (Lama Temple)

Yonghe Temple is one of the largest and most important Tibetan Buddhist temples in the world. The building and the artworks of the temple combine the Han and Tibetan styles. The temple contains a 26m tall statue of the Maitreya Buddha, the biggest existed wood carved statue of Buddha in China.

3.29 居庸关云台

云台是居庸关关城内一座汉白玉砌筑的高台，始建于元至正二年（1342），是典型的元代过街塔建筑。

Yun Tai

Yun Tai (Cloud Platform), a white marble hathpace inside Juyongguan Pass, was built in Zhizheng 2 (1342). It has a typical style of basement of cross-street pagoda in the Yuan Dynasty.

3.30　十三陵神道石像生

石像生是陵前放置的石雕人、兽，象征皇帝生前的仪威以及死后仍可主宰一切。明十三陵神道两侧排列着24只石兽和12个石人。

Stone figures, Ming Tombs

Stone figures, composed of humans or animals which were made of stone and placed along the Spectre Avenue, symbolized the imperatorial and dignified manner, as well as the domination of everything after death. There are 24 stone animals and 12 stone human figures on both sides of the Spectre Avenue of Ming Tombs.

第四单元
百姓生活

Daily Life

祁老太爷什么也不怕，只怕庆不了八十大寿。在他的壮年，他亲眼看见八国联军怎样攻进北京城。后来，他看见了清朝的皇帝怎样退位，和接续不断的内战；一会儿九城的城门紧闭，枪声与炮声日夜不绝；一会儿城门开了，马路上又飞驰着得胜的军阀的高车大马。战争没有吓倒他，和平使他高兴。逢节他要过节，遇年他要祭祖，他是个安分守己的公民，只求消消停停的过着不至于愁吃愁穿的日子。即使赶上兵荒马乱，他也自有办法：最值得说的是他的家里老存着全家够吃三个月的粮食与咸菜。这样，即使炮弹在空中飞，兵在街上乱跑，他也会关上大门，再用装满石头的破缸顶上，便足以消灾避难。

——老舍《四世同堂》

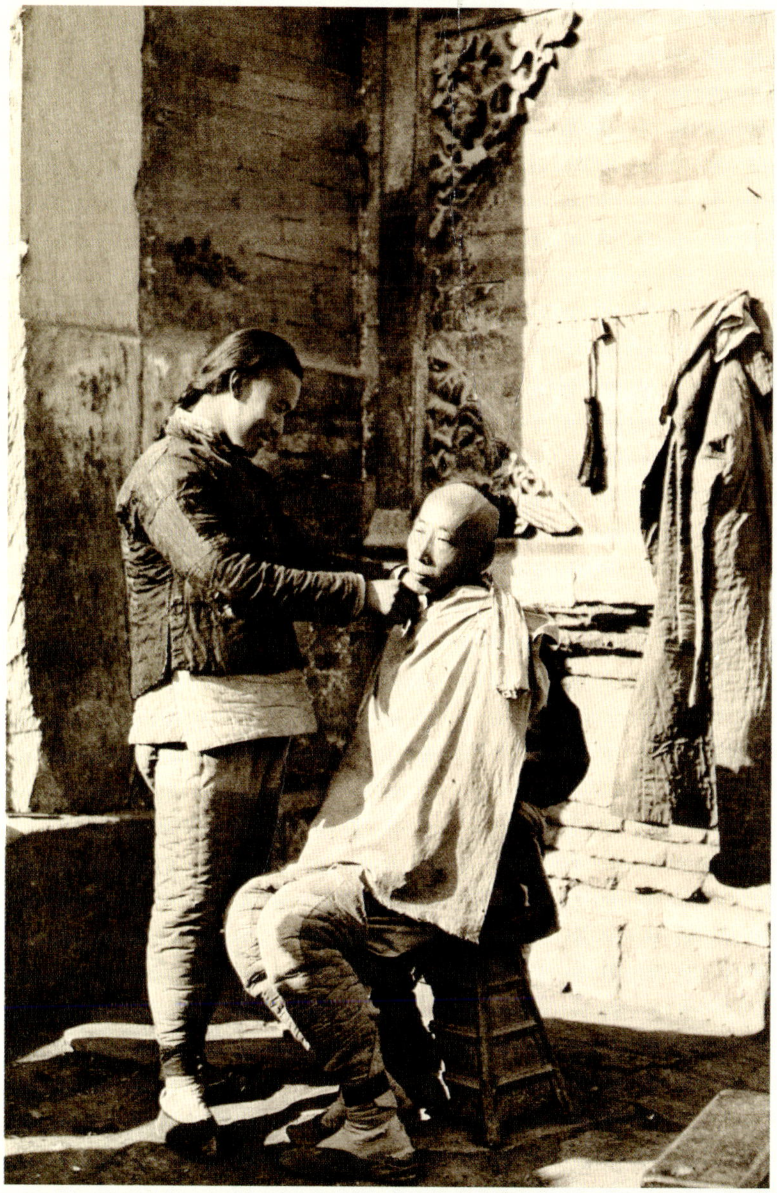

4.1 剃头匠

自清代起，剃头就是一种人们日常生活不可缺少的行业，剃头匠遍布全城大街小巷，除了有固定的剃头棚之外，更多的是“剃头挑子”。

Barber

Barber has been indispensable in people's daily life since Qing Dynasty (1644-1911). Besides barber's sheds, there were many barber carrying-poles in the streets.

4.2 万寿寺前的满族妇女

照片中间的女子穿着典型的旗装。满族妇女通常着旗装，梳“两把头”，天足，穿花盆底鞋。

Manchu-women in front of Wanshou Temple

The woman in the middle is wearing typical traditional Manchu attire. Manchu women usually wore traditional Manchu dress while they had their own hairstyle, called “Qi Tou”. Different from Han women, Manchu women didn’t bind their feet but wore flower-pot shoes.

4.3 街头食挑

照片中展现的是老北京街头食挑，根据其装备来看像是卖馄饨等热汤食的挑子。

Cookshop keeper

In the street of old Beijing there were many food vendors. According to the carrier, it seems like a Wonton vendor or a hot soup vendor.

4.4 小商贩

老北京街头常有人摆摊售卖瓜果蔬菜，这种小本生意仅能勉强维持生计，像照片里的小贩，撑一把破烂不堪的伞，可见其生活窘迫。

Dealer

It was usual to find some people selling vegetables and fruits along the street. Vendors could only earn a living with such small business. Many vendors had a tough life, just like the dealer with a broken umbrella in the photograph.

4.5 买东西的老妇

照片里的买东西的老妇前面摆着一个卖冰糖葫芦的小摊。时至今日，冰糖葫芦一直是老百姓喜爱的小吃之一，而串街叫卖糖葫芦的营生也成为一种至今不衰的行业。

Old Chinese woman shopping

In front of the old woman, it is a stall for selling sugar-coated haws. Nowadays the stick of sugar-coated haws has been one of the most popular snaps in Beijing.

4.6 人力车

人力车19世纪末由日本传入中国，也叫洋车。照片中展示的是一个人力车的聚集地。当时人力车始发站被称为“车口儿”，最大的一个“车口儿”就位于正阳门火车站。

Rickshaw stand

Rickshaw was a mode of human-powered transport originated from Japan. This photograph shows a rickshaw stand. At that time the biggest rickshaw stand located near the Zhengyangmen Railway Station.

4.7 清末民初街景

City view

4.8 拜年

春节是中国人最重要的节日，男人们大年初一串门拜年的习俗由来已久。按老北京规矩，年初一是本家同宗拜年，然后才是姻亲、朋友、同事之间拜年。

New Year's greeting

Chinese New Year, often called Spring Festival, is the most important traditional holiday. The first day of Chinese New Year is the time when families visit the oldest and most senior members of their extended family. After this they give New Year's greeting to their affinities, friends and colleagues.

4.9 弹三弦的人

三弦是老北京曲艺表演中一种比较常见的传统乐器，在北京，各种鼓书都以三弦作为主要的伴奏乐器，三弦与鼓搭配的演唱形式称作“北京单弦”。

Lute player

This is a Chinese lute, a three-stringed fretless plucked musical instrument, called San Xian. It is primarily used as a main accompanying instrument in fork arts of Beijing, as well as in ensembles and orchestras of traditional Chinese instruments.

4.10　弹月琴的人

月琴是老北京曲艺表演中另一种比较常见的传统乐器，从阮演变而来，取其形圆似月、声如琴，故名“月琴”。在京剧文场中，月琴和京胡、京二胡合称三大件。

Lute player

Yue Qin is a traditional Chinese string instrument. It is a lute with a round, hollow wooden body which gives it the nickname moon guitar. In Peking Opera, Yue Qin plays an important part as an accompanying instrument.

4.11　清理河道
Silt-removing

4.12　乞讨盲妇

乞讨在北京是一种古老的职业。照片中是一位盲人老妇，她面前摆着的笸箩是用来装别人施舍的钱物。

Blind woman beggar

Since early times beggar had became a profession in Beijing. In front of the blind woman beggar there is a little basket in order to receive benefactions.

4.13 乡下人
Peasant

4.14 绱鞋的妇人

照片中的妇人正在绱鞋。绱鞋是将纳好的鞋底与做好的鞋帮缝在一起的工艺。

Cobble woman

The woman in the photo is sewing shoes. In Chinese this step of shoes making is called "Shang". "Shang" means the combination of sole and uppers of shoes.

4.15 城外石道

老北京内外城的道路基本以土路为主，只有部分主要干道为石板铺路。然而，在动荡年代中，石道年久失修，坑洼不平，百姓更情愿走道旁的土路。

On the old flagging road

In spite of a few flagging avenues, the majority of roads in Beijing were rammed down with soil. Due to the revolutionary period, the flagstones had been seriously broken and lacked maintenance.

4.16　卸船

北京地区较为大型的漕运码头为通州张家湾码头和积水潭码头。照片中为正在卸船的北京漕运码头，从船的大小判断，此地应为较小的码头。

Loaded junk

Zhangjiawan Dock (Tongzhou District) and Jishuitan Dock (Xicheng District) were two main docks of the canal for grain transportation in old Beijing. This photo shows a loading junk at a little dock.

4.17 出殡

出殡是中国传统丧葬礼仪中的重要环节，丧事办得是否体面主要在于出殡。一般人家用八人杠，富户人家则用十六杠以上。

Chinese funeral

The photo shows the most important step in a traditional Chinese funeral, called "Chu Bin". The family employed some people to carry the coffin to the cemetery. The number of employees varied according to the social position and wealth of a family.

4.18 制秤人

在传统手工制作杆秤的工艺中，制定重量刻度是最精细的一个步骤，在确定好定盘星位置后，就用“雷公钻”对着记号开始“钻星子”，一般承受15公斤的秤要钻近300个眼。

Scale maker

The scale maker is marking the graduation with a special drill, called Leigong Drill. This is the most difficult step of scale-making.

4.19　食摊前的百姓

Refreshment stall with Manchu people

4.20 苦力

清末民初，很多穷苦的百姓靠给富户或外国人做粗活来养家糊口，他们被称为苦力。

Coolies

Coolies were a historical term for manual labourers or slaves during the 19th century and early 20th century.

4.21　戏曲艺人

照片为旦角扮相的戏曲艺人。以往戏曲里的旦角都是由男性来扮演，民国以后提倡文明新风，开创女伶与男演员同台演出的新风气。

Opera actor

In the past the female role in a performance was often played by actor. After the 1911 Revolution of China, new artists advocated allowing women to play in Peking Opera, so actresses and actors could perform together.

4.22 乡间茶馆

老北京人嗜茶，茶馆遍布京城各处。在茶馆，不仅可以饮茶，又可供生意人聚会、文人交往。茶馆种类繁多，如清茶馆、书茶馆、棋茶馆以及季节性的临时茶棚等。

Tea-house

In the past Beijing people preferred gathering in the tea-house in free time. Besides drinking tea, the tea-house was a social communication place. There were many different sorts of tea-house in Beijing, such as the one with books, with chests and with performance. Even the seasonal tea-stall could be found in the countryside.

4.23 夜间小摊贩
Cookshop keeper at night

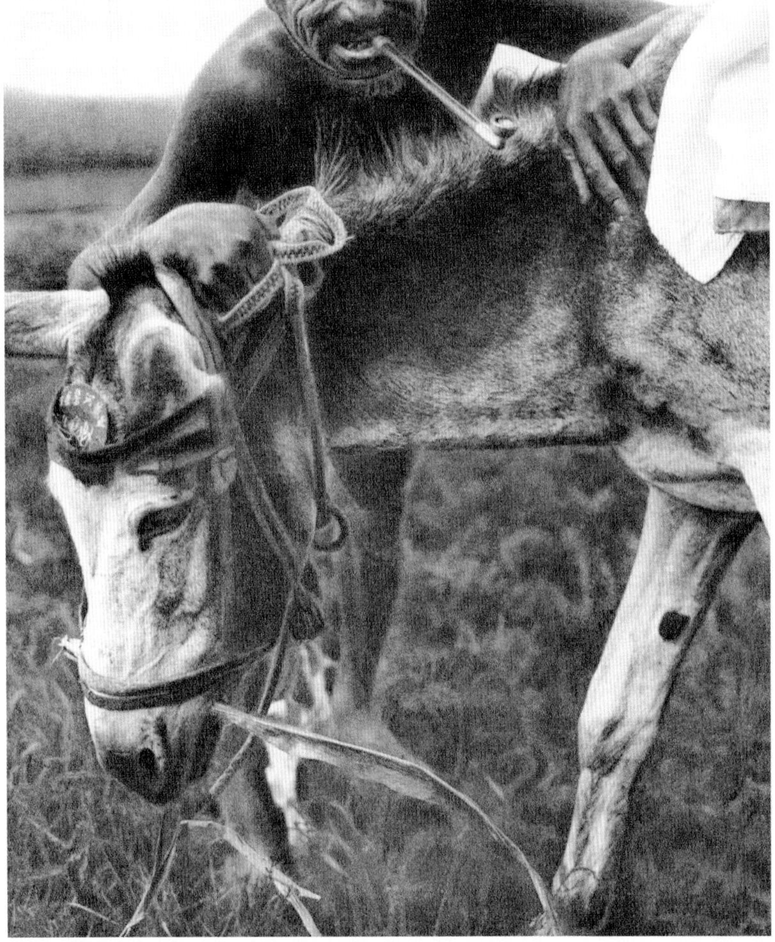

4.24 赶脚儿的

此为老北京的七十二行之一，类似今天的出租车。赶脚的把驴拴于城根，有需要者就骑上它，赶脚儿的紧随其后。

Donkey owner

The donkey in old Beijing is similar to taxi of our time. The donkeys were tied to the city wall. The guests could ride the donkeys when they needed, and paid the donkey owners who ran after the donkeys.

中国历史年表

朝代		起讫年代	都城	今地
唐		618-907	长安	陕西西安
宋	北宋	960-1127	开封	河南开封
	南宋	1127-1279	临安	浙江临安
金		1115-1234	会宁	黑龙江阿城
			中都	北京
			开封	河南开封
元		1206-1368	大都	北京
明		1368-1644	南京	江苏南京
			北京	北京
清		1616-1911	北京	北京
中华民国		1912-1949	南京	江苏南京
中华人民共和国1949年10月1日成立,首都北京。				

Chronology

Dynasty		Time	Capital	Location
Tang		618-907	Chang'an	Xi'an, Shaanxi Province
Song	Northern Song	960-1127	Kaifeng	Kaifeng, Henan Province
	Southern Song	1127-1279	Lin'an	Lin'an, Zhejiang Province
Jin		1115-1234	Huining	Acheng, Heilongjiang Province
			Zhongdu	Beijing
			Kaifeng	Kaifeng, Henan Province
Yuan		1206-1368	Dadu	Beijing
Ming		1368-1644	Nanjing	Nanjing, Jiangsu Province
			Beijing	Beijing
Qing		1616-1911	Beijing	Beijing
Republic of China		1912-1949	Nanjing	Nanjing, Jiangsu Province
On October 1st, 1949 the People's Republic of China was established. Beijing is the capital.				

地名索引
Grazetteer Name Index

英文题名索引
English Title Index